RANGER RICK'S BEST FRIENDS

HI, I'M RANGER RICK, the official conservation symbol for young members of the National Wildlife Federation, and leader of the Ranger Rick Nature Clubs. On behalf of all the animals in Deep Green Wood, welcome to our world of nature and wildlife.

The Opossums

by Anne LaBastille

**Created and Published by
The National Wildlife Federation
Washington, D. C.**

1 Zelda Possum Cleans Up

based on characters developed by J. A. Brownridge

"Hurry up, Rick," called Ollie Otter as he ran down the trail. "We can't be late for the meeting with Zelda Possum!"

Ranger Rick tried to catch up with his friend. Ahead of him on the trail patches of mud and brown grass were showing through the snow. The March sun felt hot, and it seemed that winter was just about over. "Hey, Ollie," Rick puffed, "wait up. Do you think it's warm enough to go for a swim?"

"There's only one way to find out," Ollie answered when they reached the bank of Clear Creek. "Last one in's a Wally Wolf!" And with that he took a flying leap over the edge, down the steep bank on his favorite slide, and into the water.

Rick peered over, expecting to see Ollie swimming in the clear, cold creek. Instead, Ollie was sitting in scummy, shallow water with weeds and plants draped over his head and around his neck.

"Wow, this is terrible," sputtered Ollie. "None of this stuff was here last year. What in the world has happened to Clear Creek?"

"Maybe that's what Nurse Zelda Possum wanted to see us about," said Rick.

Just then Billy Bass poked his pale face up from the surface of the water. "I'm sure glad to see you guys," he gas- ped. "I asked Zelda Possum for some help the other day because the water's so bad and I can't breathe. She suggested we all get together to talk about the water problem."

From overhead, the voice of Wise Old Owl chimed in. "You sure do have a problem," he said. "I've flown all over the territory and I've seen lots of rivers clogged up like this creek. This may be too big a problem even for Zelda."

Rick looked up from the bank and shook his head. "I think she'll know what to do. And we can all help. Opossums have so many children and take such good care of them that they make

excellent nurses."

"We'll see, Rick," said Zelda, who had come bustling out of the woods. Immediately she began to examine Billy. "I'm afraid you're not any better," she concluded. "I think you need a rest in some clear water. You'll have to go upstream past Big Town. Once you get some more oxygen you'll feel a lot better."

"I think I'll go visit my cousin Timothy Trout up in the mountains," said Billy. "But the water is cold and fast up there and I'm not used to that. Can anything be done about this mess so I can stay home?"

"People can use good old-fashioned

soap or a detergent that doesn't have phosphates," said Zelda. "That's what I use and my towels are still white and clean. I wish more people would use soap powders or detergents without phosphates. It's the phosphates that make all these plants grow so fast. Then, when the plants and algae die and decompose, oxygen in the water is used up. If only manufacturers would look harder for detergents without phosphates... then our water wouldn't be messed up and Billy wouldn't have to stay away from home so long."

As they stood on the bank sadly waving good-bye to Billy Bass, Rick heard a splash in a puddle behind him. He turned around just as Wally Wolf came crashing toward them.

"Look out!" cried Rick and clambered up the nearest tree.

Ollie turned like a flash and leaped back into the dirty creek.

Poor old Zelda Possum couldn't move very fast and Wally saw his chance for a good meal. As he ran toward her, Zelda's feet got tangled up and she tripped and toppled over the bank of the stream.

Wally tried to stop, but his feet landed in a mud puddle and he skidded toward Ollie's slide. Down he went, head over heels, into the slimy water.

Rick came down the tree and ran to the bank. As he looked down he couldn't help laughing. Wally was out in the middle of the stream with Ollie sitting on his head. Furiously, the wolf tried to get rid of him. His teeth snapped savagely as he swam toward the other shore. Slime and weeds trailed behind him and Ollie pushed him underwater as often as he could. Just before they reached the other bank, Ollie jumped off and swam quickly back toward Rick.

"Ollie, do you see Zelda?" Rick called.

"Here I am, Rick," answered Zelda from just below the edge. "I grabbed this root as I fell."

"Oh, I'm sure glad to see you," said Rick as he helped her climb back up the bank.

They looked across the stream where Wally Wolf was still sputtering and snarling at them. He tried to be fierce, but only managed to appear ridiculous, all draped in plants and slime. With one last snarl, he disappeared into the woods.

"It will be a while before he gets himself cleaned up from that mess," said Ollie.

"I hope he doesn't use one of the high phosphate detergents," giggled Zelda.

Then the three friends scampered back to Zelda's home, where all of her opossum children were amazed to see Ollie so messed up. But Zelda told them not to make fun of him. Then she found some good old-fashioned soap for Ollie in her closet. Soon he had himself clean and ready for more action.

"If plain old soap works so well," asked Ollie, "why don't people use it or the detergents without phosphates?"

"Because most people don't know that phosphate detergents are bad. That's where your Rangers may be able to help, Rick," Zelda said. "They can tell their parents and their friends to use regular soap."

Then she turned to her children and told them how Billy Bass had been forced to leave his home because of the phosphate detergents. The children felt very sorry for Billy and jumped into Zelda's pouch where the world always seemed safe and secure to them.

"No harm's going to come to them in there, Zelda," Ollie laughed.

"That's right, Zelda," Rick added. "You know lots of tricks for keeping animals safe and healthy. I think our readers would like to know more about you opossums and how you manage to survive so well. From the next chapter of this book they can learn something about you and your family."

2 Growing Up An Opossum

isn't easy, but Oppy
(whom you'll meet in the next chapter)
and the other pouch babies
are eager to go—
especially at night.

Dinner's always ready in mother's pouch for six-week-old opossums.

He was Number 15. Mother Opossum named him and his 14 brothers and sisters for the letters of the alphabet, all the way from Abraham to Nancy. Then came Oppy, the littlest and the last.

Oppy passed the first test of his life but not all his brothers and sisters were so lucky. He safely made the trip up to his mother's pouch from her belly where he had been born. He climbed up through the thick, wet fur after his bigger brothers and sisters, and slipped down into the pouch. There he found a nipple full of warm milk. He held on for dear life. He would not let go for weeks and weeks.

None of the little opossums could see yet. Each one was smaller than a honeybee or the beans your mother uses to make chili. Their legs were tiny stubs with claws.

At the end of the first month Oppy poked his head outside. Near the end of the second month he and all his sisters and brothers began creeping out of the pouch. Soon they would tumble back. They were as large as mice now and had hair, yet could still not fend for themselves.

Mama 'Possum's pouch gave them safety, warmth, food, and free rides. Because it's so convenient, you'd think other animals might want a pouch. But it's a feature that belongs only to marsupials—a family of animals that includes kangaroos and koala bears and opossums. And the only marsupials in North America are opossums.

As they grew older, Oppy and the whole bunch would climb out and go for trips on top of Mama. Each one would hang onto her fur or her tail. The little opossums were not so smart as bobcats, deer, or bears, but they quickly learned to use the different parts of their bodies.

At three months, opossum babies ride mother's back and learn to hunt.

than any other land animal in North America.)

One night when they were about three months old Oppy and his brothers and sisters went for a ride with Mama. It was raining hard. They had to cross a stream to get back home. The water was so swift

Oppy found he could use his tail like a fifth arm and hand. It would curl around branches or hold things. He also tried out his big toes: they worked almost like thumbs on human hands. They helped Oppy pick fruit and grab worms. Best of all were his teeth—50 sharp white ones! (Opossums have more teeth

12

and deep that some of the baby opossums were pulled off her back. Oppy was one of them. It was sink or swim. To his surprise he kept afloat and finally reached shore.

But his mother, sisters, and brothers were gone. He had been swept far away. Once he thought he heard his sister crying, but it was only a night bird. Oppy was dripping wet and cold. How he wished to be back in his mother's warm pouch!

Oppy climbed a tree to see where he was. It was all new country. He was on his own. Would he be able to find food and defend himself?

Beneath a pile of rocks he found a dry nook. With his tail he carried dry leaves inside for a bed. After a couple of days Oppy was used to being alone. He no longer missed his family.

It was summer and there was lots to eat. One night while he was in a tree munching on apples he felt a heavy blow behind him. A huge horned owl just missed him, but knocked him to the ground. He lay quietly for a long time. When he got to his feet, his whole body ached.

Young opossums find tree climbing easy. No wonder: They use long fingers, sharp claws, and a tail for balancing or hanging.

But he limped home. He was tough and would survive.

His next lesson in life came that fall. Oppy was about the size of a house cat now. The young opossum found a farm nearby and killed a chicken. It was easier than hunting wild birds. Just as he started to eat, a young fox ran up. Oppy didn't

Facing an angry farmer, the opossum below defends his catch—a chicken.

Above: A young opossum on his own has just discovered his favorite food—persimmons. That one's not quite ripe. He'd better reach for another. *Left:* There's something else worth checking: a box turtle, but he's hiding inside his shell.

15

A swim is more than an outing for young opossums; it's a lesson in staying alive (*above*).
So is a meeting with a hawk (*right*); mother shows how to hiss and bare sharp teeth.

care to fight the fox, but he did want his dinner. Once Oppy's mother had hissed when a hawk attacked and the hawk had flown away. So now he curled his lips, showed all his teeth, and hissed as loud as he could. The fox jumped back in alarm, turned tail, and ran away!

Oppy enjoyed his chicken.

The winter was very cold. Oppy stayed home on zero nights because his naked, ratlike tail and thin hairless ears might freeze. On warmer days he came out of his new den to look for food. Gone were the juicy berries, persimmons,

baby birds, grapes, worms, corn, frogs, pawpaws, insects, and apples of summer and fall. Now the opossum had to hunt hard for a few mice, acorns, garbage and even for dead animals. He searched everywhere and ate almost anything.

One night he found a dead rabbit on a road. Oppy was so hungry he began to eat. Suddenly he heard a roaring noise coming toward him. It was coming very fast. In terror he rolled over to the side of the road and lay still. The noise turned into a huge shiny blue animal. It had four round legs and ran very fast. (A

Two tricks has a 'possum
    When foxes are near:
To climb to a treetop
    Or hiss full of fear.

But when these two fail
    He tries something instead:
Rolls up like a ball
    And pretends that he's dead.

18

car, of course, though Oppy didn't know it.)

The roaring stopped. Two people got out of the car and walked over to Oppy. He played dead. The little girl was sad because she thought the car had killed the opossum.

The huge animal started roaring again and ran away. Oppy stood up. He felt fine. His trick had worked. Playing dead was the best way to stay alive.

When spring came Oppy met a large female opossum. For a while she stayed with Oppy as his mate. But Oppy really didn't like company. And the female wanted to go back to her own den. One night she left just the way she had come.

Oppy would never see his mate again or her babies. He would not be there to defend the female if she was attacked by hawks or owls. He could not carry the young because he did not have a pouch. She would do everything herself.

Oppy didn't mind. That's the way 'possums are.

3 The Wild Orphans

What do you do when you find a run-over opossum with nine surviving children? Well, if you're like a friend of ours, you ask seven neighbors to help out by each taking one of the tiny babies; then you do your best to help nurse the last two.

Our friend's three children were glad to help, too. They laughed when the opossum babies tried to find a pouch in the lap of a person who held them. They felt terrible when the opossum babies grew weak and wouldn't drink much of the milk from their feeding bottles.

But soon a diet was fixed up. By

the time the opossums' three-month birthday came around, it looked as if they'd live. Then the children played with them more easily and studied them more closely: the leathery ears, the soft fur, the strong pink tail used for an extra support. But there was no way to teach them a trick; no way to get them to answer when called by name.

One day our friend and his family went to New York City. They took the opossums along to Central Park. In the picture at left a boy who walked by looks astonished. "What kind of a funny-looking wild animal is that?" he asked.

The children explained that it was an orphan opossum, one of the two they'd raised. And they promised that they would soon be letting the animals go, because now the opossums no longer needed care.

A few days later they released their opossum friends into the woods. "They sure were nice pets," one of the children sighed.

"No. They weren't pets," another said.

"They didn't even look back," added the third. "But, anyway... goodbye!"

4 Look Out For Possumnappers!

based on characters developed by J. A. Brownridge

Spring had come once more to Deep Green Wood. The trees were green again, April rains had brought clean water to Shady Pond, and there was a feeling of happiness and excitement everywhere.

Ranger Rick was enjoying a long and peaceful nap in his cozy den. But he stirred restlessly as some of the new young residents of Deep Green Wood began to play outside his door, squealing and chattering.

All the wildlife was up and moving about after a long winter. Those that hibernated and those that just took extra-long naps were scurrying here and there looking for food. The birds that had migrated to the warm southland were back and looking for good nesting places.

There was a steady hum of conversation as old friends met and exchanged stories of their adventures and travels.

"Wake up, Rick," came a loud and piercing voice.

Yawning sleepily, Rick poked his head out the door and saw Ollie Otter. "All right," he said, "it *is* a lovely day and I shouldn't waste it."

Down the trail the two friends romped. They greeted and chattered with many old friends. Everyone was glad to see Rick.

Everything seemed wonderful until they rounded a bend in the trail. A short distance ahead they saw Zelda Possum talking excitedly with a group of other Deep Green Wood mothers. Mrs. Bear, Mrs. Squirrel, Mrs. Skunk, Mrs. Rabbit, and Mrs. Bluebird seemed very upset to hear Mrs. Possum's news.

"Hey, what's going on?" called Rick. "You folks don't seem as happy as everyone else."

"Oh, Rick," they replied. "Are we glad to see you! We just don't know what's happening. Zelda Possum has just told us she's lost three of her children."

"Have you hunted for them?" asked Rick.

"Of course we have," growled Mrs. Bear. "We've looked all over the place and there's not a trace of them."

"Has anyone seen Wally Wolf around?" asked Ollie, looking nervously over his shoulder.

"There hasn't been a sign of him either," Mrs. Bluebird chirped sadly.

"We'll start a search for them right away," said Rick. "You keep looking too and we'll meet you back at headquarters at noon."

Away trotted Rick and Ollie, no longer happy and carefree. They were serious and very cautious as they peered around each bend in the trail. Every hiding place the two could remember was searched. Not a sign of the missing young ones was found.

Finally they reached Shady Pond.

"You swim across and search the other side of the pond," ordered Rick. "I'll continue on this side and we'll meet half way."

Ollie was delighted at the chance to get in a little swimming. He dove into the pond like a brown arrow and was soon out on the other side, happily shaking off a big spray of water. He looked back longingly at the pond, but a loud call from Rick reminded him of his serious business and he dashed off into the woods.

Rick moved cautiously ahead on his side of the pond, looking into every clump of bushes, every hollow log and every cave he could find.

Suddenly he heard strange noises up ahead. Loud thumpings and muffled screams came from just over a hill. Very slowly and carefully Rick poked his head over the rise to see what was making the strange racket.

What he saw puzzled him even more than what he had heard. Right in the middle of the trail he saw a box bouncing up and down, but no one was near it. All the noise was coming from the box.

"What in the world..." Rick wondered to himself. Then suddenly he recognized the sounds. It was Ollie Otter calling for help from inside the box.

Quickly but cautiously Rick crept up to the box. "Ollie?" he called softly.

But still the wild bumping and yelling continued. "Ollie!" Rick shouted sharply and banged on the outside of the box.

"Oh, Rick!" came the frantic though muffled voice of Ollie. "I'm trapped. Please hurry and get me out of here."

"Just keep calm for a few minutes and I'll have you out," said Rick soothingly. All the time he was speaking he was looking around for tools to work with.

He saw a fallen tree limb and spotted a large rock. He quickly put the rock beside the box and pushed one end of the tree limb under the box and over the rock. Then, straining mightily on the other end of the limb, he forced the box up off the ground.

In a few seconds Ollie was free and the two companions ran back into the woods.

"What happened?" asked Rick.

"Well," said Ollie. "I saw some food under that box, but as soon as I picked it up, the whole thing dropped and I couldn't get out."

"I'm surprised that you'd get caught by an old trap like that," said Rick. "It solves the mystery of the young opossums. I guess some children have become possumnappers! They're trapping the opossums and taking them home for pets.

"I'll have to get Ranger Tom to talk to them and see if something can't be done to protect our young ones."

Off went Rick to see Ranger Tom. When Tom heard the story he went to the people of Big Town and explained the trouble they might be making for themselves. He explained that wild animals are always wild. Little opossums may be cute and fun when small. But they do grow up, and they may bite or claw the children who try to tame them. They don't make good pets.

The young trappers had not realized another reason why baby animals should not be taken from their mothers.

Mrs. Possum and the other animal mothers train their young to find food and to protect themselves from enemies. Those that do not get this training and are then released in the wild often starve to death. Or they are quickly caught by their enemies and eaten.

Tom also reminded the people of Big Town that it is against the law in most places to capture and keep wild animals. Even professional wildlife-management people must get special permits for this.

When the Big Town parents and children realized what they had done, the possumnappers returned their captives to Deep Green Wood, where they belonged. Zelda Possum invited everyone over to her house for a picnic to celebrate. The animal families were happy to be back together again.

Rick was very grateful to Ranger Tom. And from then on the parents of Big Town warned their children that—regardless of television shows they had seen or stories they had read—all wild animals can be dangerous, even when they are as cute as opossums.

5
Cousins Across the Ocean

This Australian cuscus looks so much like a Virginia opossum it's hard to believe it isn't Oppy himself, living Down Under.

AUSTRALIA has lots of animals that we call possums—though they really aren't. But when Captain James Cook, who discovered Australia, first saw these marsupials, they reminded him of the opossum he'd seen in Virginia; and so the name.

People who know animals inside and out say that Australian possums, really phalangers (faLANjers), are only distant cousins. They had a common ancestor with the Virginia opossum millions of years ago.

As a matter of fact, there are lots of Australian marsupials who are Oppy's distant cousins: kangaroos, wombats, and koala bears to name just a few. But only the cuscus (KUSSkuss) and some phalangers look like Oppy.

Smaller Australian phalangers (*above*) look a bit like mice. Others with webbing from wrist to ankle look like flying squirrels; they even have the squirrel's bushy tail.

But most phalangers have hands, feet, and tails that are good for climbing and grasping. And the ones who hunt at night have Oppy's beautiful big eyes.

Perhaps someday you will go to Australia and see Oppy's distant relatives. Next: a look at Oppy's close relatives in South America.

SOUTH AND CENTRAL AMERICA have more genuine opossums and more different kinds of opossums than any other place on earth. The opossums have been there since the days of the dinosaurs and are among the world's oldest mammals.

The opossum you are most apt to see South of the Border is truly Oppy's twin (*right*): eyes big, nose pointed, ears leathery, feet and tail good for climbing. Like Oppy he has coarse fur of long guard hairs and is the size of a cat. Indeed, he is so much like Oppy, he would probably have to wear a sombrero for you to tell them apart.

The yapok, also a South American opossum, has short fur, webbed feet, and a body streamlined for swimming.

The yapok's pouch is watertight, but many South American opossums have no pouch at all. The babies just hang on.

Most South of the Border opossums are tiny and mouselike. Occasionally Central America ships a stowaway to the United States by chance when a little fellow gets carried away while eating bananas.

Trailing the Opossum

The next time it snows or the ground gets muddy, look for star-shaped tracks. They are the tell-tale sign of the opossum, who has five finger-like toes on every foot. You will probably also see the faint line he draws, dragging his down-curled tail behind him as he waddles along the trail.

When John Smith brought the first boatloads of colonists to Virginia in 1607, the opossum lived only in the South. But since the beginning of this century, each opossum, in his short life, has wandered farther from home. As woodland has become more open, the opossum has spread out across North America, going up into New England and Canada, across the Great Plains, and down into Texas.

Parts of the West he seems to have avoided; possibly it is too dry. But he has turned up in Washington, Oregon, and California, showing up in such numbers in Los Angeles that 1,000 opossums were picked up in Hollywood in one year.

The hind foot of the opossum (*right*) is like a little hand, with four long-nailed fingers and a thumb.

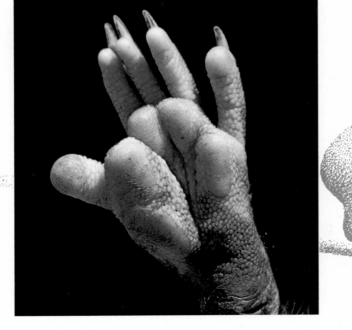

WHEN YOU SEE AN OPOSSUM...

for the first time, you'll be surprised at its tricks—even if it isn't a mother opossum with a half dozen baby opossums hanging onto her back. The opossum is big and furry, about the size of a house cat, and usually light gray, although occasionally you may chance to see one that is much darker.

The opossum's face is pale. The eyes, large and shiny, stand out black against the light fur. A dark blaze between the eyes, and dark fur around them, makes them look even bigger and blacker.

The opossum has a pink nose, long and pointed, and black leathery ears. His toes, pink too and bare, are perfect for climbing. His front foot curls over the branch. The hind foot, with a thumb-like toe, holds on like a hand. His tail, long, pointed and scaly, helps him feel his way and keep his balance.

Trees are the opossum's favorite haunt and in these he moves with ease. On the ground, however, you will find that he waddles or trudges flat-footed on short legs, tail to one side. It curls downward when he's healthy, upward when he's ill. If he loops the tip, keep a close eye on him. He may be about to fill the loop with leaves to line his burrow.

Because the opossum is a nocturnal animal, you will probably have to hunt for him at night, by flashlight. Check wooded areas, especially those near streams. And check your own back yard. You may discover him foraging for food in your garden or scrounging in your garbage pail.

But don't expect to see any of his friends. The opossum is a loner. And don't expect to see him often. He is a gypsy and will soon be on his way again to far places.

32